# Faith's Feather Pen

July 2017
ISBN-13:
978-1548541835

ISBN-10:
1548541834

Dedicated to my
1st & 2nd Grade classes
Of 2015 - 2107
May you always have
Inspiration and Motivation
To write...

You have a story to tell!
Love Mrs. Buske

"I don't know what to write!
H E L P!"

"You don't need help...

...You need a feather pen.
I have one just for you."

They come in different colors,
each with a different story to tell.

So close your eyes and listen
to the amazing ideas within your brain.

Enjoy the thoughts
you see and hear.

When I count to three,
repeat after me...1..2..3..

"I have a story to tell
and it starts with me!"

Now it's time to pick up your feather pen and start to write.

Maybe it's a silly story?

Or mysterious?

Are you doing something
with your friends?

Are your creative juices
ready to write?

If they're not, do not fret
you're just getting your author feet wet.

When you get stuck and
aren't sure what to write...

Remember...
You have a story to tell!

Write about what you know
And the words will flow
When challenged to write something new
Don't give up, simply follow through.

You don't *need* a feather pen,
the gift to write is IN YOU!!
The feather pen just makes it more fun!

Use the following pages to jot down your ideas for stories to write.
Don't overthink it, just write & have fun!

_____

_____

_____

_____

_____

_____

_____

_____

_____

_____